Blood is Blood

Blood is Blood

Endre Farkas &
Carolyn Marie Souaid

Signature
EDITIONS

Cover design by Doowah Design.
Cover photo by Michael Klein.
Photo of Endre Farkas by DHFoto.
Photo of Carolyn Marie Souaid by Monique Dykstra.

This book was printed on Ancient Forest Friendly paper.
Printed and bound in Canada by Marquis Book Printing Inc.

We acknowledge the support of the Canada Council for the Arts and the Manitoba Arts Council for our publishing program.

Library and Archives Canada Cataloguing in Publication

Farkas, Endre, 1948–
    Blood is Blood / Endre Farkas & Carolyn Marie Souaid.

Poems.
Accompanied by a DVD.
ISBN 978-1-897109-46-5

    I. Souaid, Carolyn Marie, 1959–   II. Title.

PS8561.A72B56 2010   C811'.54   C2010-905620-5

Signature Editions
P.O. Box 206, RPO Corydon, Winnipeg, Manitoba, R3M 3S7
www.signature-editions.com

to all those who believe
that there is another way

Introduction

When we first met in the mid-1990s at the Trois-Rivières International Poetry Festival, we spent the better part of a night talking about ourselves and our backgrounds. Looking back, we're still not sure why we clicked. Perhaps it was the atmosphere— poets from far and wide, a good table and a glut of French wine. Initially, we hedged, reluctant to be upfront. One of us was Jewish and a child of Holocaust survivors; the other, a Lebanese Christian with family still living in the "old country." But our appreciation for each other's work helped us broach the issue of our differences as writers first and as "ethnics" second.

In due course, we became friends and discussed the idea of working together on various projects. We both had a desire to create, contribute to and engage our community — the writing community, not the familial/cultural/religious one. Our early collaborations involved moving poetry off the page and onto the stage. We put poems on city buses and produced Montreal's only cabaret of performance-based poetry.

In December 2005, we joined a delegation of Canadian poets invited to Paris to participate in the 4th Symposium Against Isolation and Torture. For the event, we created a two-voice text based on the words of prisoners of conscience whose diary entries had been smuggled out of Turkish jails. In Paris, we encountered many Middle Eastern delegates and engaged in some heated discussions about Israel and the Arab world.

The next summer, a new war erupted in Lebanon. As the tensions in the Middle East escalated, the deep-seated cultural baggage from our respective families began to resurface — mostly accusations about the "other."

Poetry helped us get through what were difficult times. Writers both, we saw a literary parallel between our situation and the story of Romeo and Juliet and decided to use this conceit as a dramatic way to symbolize the conflict. We began to write back and forth as though we were the characters from the two proud houses. Across the chasm, we wrote about what was going on and how we really felt — sad, angry, bitter, loving, supportive, antagonistic, and more. Here, in the poems, we could reveal some of our dark prejudices and deal with them, rather than sweep them under the carpet.

The causes of this conflict are ancient, many and complex, and as the piece evolved over time, the text began to reflect this more and more. The Romeo and Juliet theme broadened into a more universal one. Working on the various segments, changing them, challenging their "truths" and editing, the process became truly collaborative. By the end, it was difficult for either of us to claim any one part of the text as our own.

Here in the "multicultural" West, it is easy to slip into apathy, to feel that there is nothing we can do, nothing we need to do to initiate change where change is due. But artists have an important role to play in the discussion of what unfolds on the international stage. Although *Blood is Blood* is set in the troubled Middle East, its narrative can be applied to tribal wars that have wreaked havoc around the globe: in Ireland, in the former Yugoslavia, in Russia, in Darfur, in Zimbabwe, and elsewhere.

The long poem is the script of the DVD *Blood is Blood* included in this book. The text is laid out so that the two voices face each other on the page, and to suggest the idea that the so-called enemies are, in some ways, mirror images of each other. The making of the video was an interesting process. Our challenge was to create visual images for the poetic images suggested by the text. We wanted the visuals to be an integral part of the text, to enhance rather than mimic. We experimented with multiple ways that text and image could become video-poety.

An early version of *Blood is Blood* was produced in Toronto by Steve Wadhams of CBC Radio, and aired in 2006. Since then, we have performed it in different incarnations at a number of events — at peace concerts, at interfaith gatherings, and at poetry readings — and it has often provoked a visceral reaction. Some have judged it to be too pro-Arab; others too pro-Israel. We wondered how people attending the same performance could have such different reactions! On the other hand, we take this as a good sign because it is generating real dialogue. Such dialogue is not always pretty or polite, but it is certainly preferable to political rhetoric or to "discussions" through cross hairs.

Endre Farkas
Carolyn Marie Souaid

Montreal, 2010

Hey!

I was here first!

I was!

I was!

No!

It's mine!

It's mine!

No!

I dare you to cross this line!

I double double dare you

I to infinity plus one dare you!
I dare you!

What?

No, I was here first!

I was!

I was!
No!

This is mine!

No! It's mine!

It's mine!
No!

I double dare you

I to infinity dare you

I dare you!

No, He can't!

No! My God can beat up your God!

No! He can't!
Yes, He can!

Allah!

Allah!

Allah!
Nyah nyah nyah nyah nyah!

No! I killed you!

I fixed myself up and killed you back!

Yes!

My God can beat up your God!

Yes, He can!
No! My God can beat up your God!

No! He can't
Yes, He can!

Yaweh!

Yaweh!

Yaweh!

Nyah nyah nyah nyah nyah!

I killed you!

No! I killed you first!

No, you didn't!
Yes!

Bullets.

This brutal rain,
a prologue.

We are
the Chosen

the ones who signed the covenant,
delivered the Word
and constantly argue with God.

We are the wanderers
who honour learning because it is holy
and easy to pack at a prophet's notice.

We are the seekers
of the land of milk and honey,
the volatile sunshot light nourishing the earth.

Hail.
This brutal reign.

In cross hairs — we meet.

Hail.
This brutal rain,
a prologue.

We are

the desert dwellers of the shifting dune

and the wind above its infinite wave.

We are the geniuses of zero.

We are the travellers
and traders of camphor and
cloves, myrrh and rosewater.

We are the alphabet
made phonetic,
the volatile sunshot light nourishing the earth.

Bullets.

This brutal reign.

In cross hairs — we meet.

Your people.
Your people.
Your people.
Your people.
Your proud, arrogant people
whose pyramided history
was built on my people's back.

Whose children learn early
that we are dogs and infidels
not even worthy of a left-hand handshake.

I memorize the scene
like some call to prayer.

This making and unmaking of the world.

)o(

Perhaps if we were naked

I'd trust you
and you me
and with our privates

we'd think it silly

to be aiming guns

Your people.
Your earmarked, persecuted people
whose ovens smell and will always smell of revenge
inferiority, revenge, revenge.
Your people.
Your people.
Your people.

Whose black, barbed-wire past
excuses them for making an industry of Hate,
excuses them for every slaughterhouse that ever
moved lock, stock, and barrel into their hearts.

I memorize the scene
like some call to prayer.

This making and unmaking of the world.

)o(

Perhaps if we were naked
I'd trust you

and you me
and with our privates
exposed to the wind

stupid
to be aiming guns

Your people.
Your proud, arrogant people,
whose teachers deny my roots.
Your people.
Your people.
Your people.
Your people.
Your people
whose stranglehold on their own by hate-mongering
believe it is their God-given right

I memorize the scene
like some call to prayer:

This making and unmaking of the world.

)o(

Perhaps if we were naked
you'd see me

and our tribal bravado
would be a mirage in the summer heat

Perhaps if we were naked
we'd think it absurd to make demands
to give up what no one owns.

Perhaps if we were naked
You and I could be...innocent.

ARAB

Your people.
Your people. Your people.
Your earmarked, persecuted people
whose two-for-the-price-of-one guerilla tanks,
cockroach armies, designer bombs
signed by their own children
gleefully rip the limbs off cities, cedars, babies.
Your people, whose Shylocks
and Christ-killers bargain with the devil
even on the Sabbath behind closed doors.

I memorize the scene
like some call to prayer:

This making and unmaking of the world.

)o(

Perhaps if we were naked
you'd see me

and our tribal bravado
would be a mirage in the summer heat.

Perhaps if we were naked
we'd think it absurd to make demands
to give up what no one owns.

Perhaps if we were naked
You and I could be...innocent?

Let us take an eye for an eye.
So no one sees the children die!
So no one sees the women die!
So no one sees the menfolk die!

So no one sees that blood is blood
intermingling in the sand.

Whose it is no one knows and…no one sees.
Let us take an eye for an eye until everyone is blind.

ЈОС

You flaunted your *moon.*

You took aim.
You!

Let us take an eye for an eye.
So no one sees the children die!
So no one sees the women die!
So no one sees the menfolk die!
So no one sees that blood is blood
intermingling in the sand.

Whose it is no one knows and…no one sees.
Let us take an eye for an eye until everyone is blind.

)o(

You stirred first in me
needing a country
land upon which to land
and seed   your future
uncertain

You flaunted your *star*.

You took aim.
You!

We, cruel and ignorant,
dealers in death.
Not so special,
no more Chosen than the rest.
Users of terror and torture;
secret police guarding with Uzis
camps of barbed-wire fences.

Like everyone with land to protect,
prefer the Golan Heights to the moral high ground,
become what we always were — a people
who follow visions and orders
and must be held accountable for *that*.

Ceasefire!

Cease!   Fire!

We, misogynists, fathers,
brothers.
Not so special;
keepers of women, warlords,
tribal in American pickups
aiming AK 47s at God, at brother.

Like everyone, obedient to oil-rich sheiks;
believers, trading life for a lair of virgins,
become what we always were—a people
who follow visions and orders
and must be held accountable for *that*.

Ceasefire!

Cease!   Fire!

From here

from this new world of immigrants

where we have come to forget

it is easy to see what both sides want

from this huge land of possibility

stolen, settled, owned;
here it's easy to be as wise as Solomon.

Cease!   Fire!

)0(

From this huge land of peace

we already have what we need, what we want

it's easy to say
play nice and share.

We might have met through cross hairs.

From here
not from there

patios, sunscreen, business as usual

for now

a delicate balance

ears attuned to the anytime news of sniper winds

Cease!   Fire!

)o(

In the same July sun, we link arms

ignore the grenade and walk away, heads held high.

We might have met through cross hairs.

Arab
with history tattooed to your heart and soul.
There, war is a contest of more and more,

It's easy to say

but still say

God
Damn those bombing the cradle of first-borns
in which we were lullabied
under the shade of olive trees.

God

God

God
Damn old gods made in the heart's furnace
of men who grow fat on such carnage.
May they dwell in eternal hell,
writhe in putrid agony,
forever feasted on by maggots
each bearing the face of those
who desecrate our manger.

Jew
with history tattooed to your heart and soul.
There, war is a contest of more and more,
a *dabke* of blood and brains in the ruined light.

How to say the unsayable
but still say

God

God
Damn those zealots and preachers sending home-made
rockets and hi-tech missiles across the azure heavens
for the words of their gods.

God
Damn those who splatter flesh against doors like Passover
blood, on Sabbath plates, on Persian carpets.

God

May they dwell in eternal hell,
writhe in putrid agony,
forever feasted on by maggots
each bearing the face of those
who desecrate our manger.

Games to Play:

The Ten Plagues of Passover

BLOOD:

Prepare a large pitcher, empty except for some red food colouring. Pour in water and watch it magically turn to blood!

FROGS:

Have everyone get out of his chair and hop around the room croaking like a frog.

LICE:

The toy store is a good source for animal-based plagues.

WILD ANIMALS:

Toy stores are filled with plastic lions, snakes, elephants and bears. You can put on a mask.

PESTILENCE:

If you can impersonate a dead animal, go right ahead.

BOILS:

The Egyptians were covered with open sores. Have everyone break out into an uncontrollable fit of itching.

HAIL:

Marshmallows: kosher ones work best for this.

Wartime Emergency Provisions

WATER

canned food, dried fruit and nuts, thick plastic sheets, masking tape, bandages, batteries, flashlights, blankets, cigarettes, matches, toothbrush, soap, portable radio, toilet paper, biscuits, chocolate, chewing gum, baby wipes, Barbie dolls. **Wartime Emergency Provisions**. Water, canned food, dried fruit and nuts, thick plastic sheets, masking tape, bandages, batteries, flashlights, blankets, cigarettes, matches, toothbrush, soap, portable radio, toilet paper, biscuits, chocolate, chewing gum, baby wipes, Barbie dolls. **Wartime Emergency Provisions**. Water, canned food, dried fruit and nuts, thick plastic sheets, masking tape, bandages, batteries, flashlights, blankets, cigarettes, matches, toothbrush, soap, portable radio, toilet paper, biscuits, chocolate, chewing gum, baby wipes, Barbie dolls. **Wartime Emergency Provisions**. Water, canned food, dried fruit and nuts, thick plastic sheets, masking tape, bandages, batteries, flashlights, blankets, cigarettes, matches, toothbrush, soap, portable radio, toilet paper, biscuits, chocolate, chewing gum, baby wipes, Barbie dolls. **Wartime Emergency Provisions**. Water, canned food, dried fruit and nuts, thick plastic sheets, masking tape, bandages, batteries, flashlights, blankets, cigarettes, matches, toothbrush, soap, portable radio, toilet paper, biscuits, chocolate, chewing gum, baby wipes, Barbie dolls. **Wartime Emergency Provisions**. Water, canned

LOCUSTS:
Hop. It's good exercise before the festive meal.

DARKNESS:

During the plague, Jews searched Egyptian homes for
valuables as "payment" for the many years of hard
labour. Have everyone put on a blindfold.
Make it a treasure hunt.

FIRST BORN:

We don't recommend you try this at home.

Have fun!

)o(

We are.

We are not.

We are.
We are not.
We are
our hearts, unpredictable,
lie and do not lie, do not lie and lie, lie and do not lie
on the perilous border.

food, dried fruit and nuts, thick plastic sheets, masking tape, bandages, batteries, flashlights, blankets, cigarettes, matches, toothbrush, soap, portable radio, toilet paper

One sealed room, windows painted black.

INCARCERATION

)o(

We are not.
We are.
We are not.
We are.

We are not.
We are
our hearts, unpredictable,
do not lie and lie, lie and do not lie, lie and do not lie
on the perilous border.

Separate

we navigate the space between cedars,
between points of stars.

We become shadows
chasing shadows
into infinity.

)o(

While the fight for a scant strip of land drones on…

a pairing for the new world.

Bold-faced, we stand
on our fledgling speck of earth.

We eat, breathe;
we watch light beget light,

the glorious molecules dovetailing.

Side by side
we navigate the space between cedars,
between points of stars.

We become shadows
chasing shadows
 into infinity.

)o(

We germinate in the chromosomes of a human century:

a pairing for the new world.

Bold-faced, we stand
on our fledgling speck of earth.

We breathe, sleep;
we watch light beget light,

the glorious molecules dovetailing.

The sun and moon
what cosmos they were
in and out and of
whose scent
who was breathing
who was in whom
it was impossible to know
entwined.

A moon.

A man.
A woman.
To seed the garden.

)o(

You are the mystic lyre.

You are the flowering sky —
saffron, carmine, lilac and more.

You are the dream asleep
curled about the prophesized word.

Kin
I am skin
and

Entwined
it was impossible to know
who was in whom
who was breathing
whose scent
in and out and of
what cosmos they were
the sun and moon.

A sun.

A man.
A woman.
To seed the garden.

)o(

You are the mystic lute.

You are the flowering sky —
saffron, carmine, lilac and more.

You are the dream asleep
curled about the prophesized word.

Kin

and
I am breath.

Listen —

To say I love you
is to commit high treason

but love so often does.

To say I love you
is to leave all senses behind
but love so often does.

To say I love you
is to be exiled from the garden
but love so often is.

To say I love you
is to go insane

but love so often doesn't.

Listen —

To say I love you
is to go against all reason
but love so often does.

To say I love you
is to travel blind

but love so often does.

To say I love you
is to be exiled from the desert
but love so often is.

To say I love you
may be the only way to end this game

but love so often doesn't.

One is enough!

One dead Arab breaks my heart
because it breaks you.

One is too many.
And Goddamn it
one is never enough!

One is enough!

One dead Jew breaks my heart
because it breaks you.

One is too many.
And Goddamn it
one is never enough!

On our separate balconies

loving the beauty of the night.

Crescent moon in the heavens

On our separate balconies
loving the beauty of the night.

Wishes upon shooting stars.

The arc of rockets.

Wishes.

The reign of death upon us all.

On our separate balconies

loving the beauty of the night.

Shining star in the heavens.

On our separate balconies
loving the beauty of the night.

Wishes upon shooting stars.

The arc of rockets.

Wishes.

The reign of death upon us all.

Let us take an eye for an eye until everyone is blind.

Let us take an eye for an eye until everyone is blind.

ENDRE FARKAS was born in Hungary and is a child of Holocaust survivors. He and his parents escaped during the 1956 uprising and settled in Montreal. His work has always had a political consciousness and has always pushed the boundaries of poetry. Since the 1970s, he has collaborated with dancers, musicians and actors to move the poem from page to stage.

Still at the forefront of the Quebec English language literary scene —writing, editing, publishing and performing— Farkas is the author of eleven books, including *Quotidian Fever: New and Selected Poems (1974-2007)*. He is the two-time regional winner of the CBC Poetry "Face Off" Competition. His play, *Haunted House*, based on the life and work of the poet A.M. Klein, was produced in Montreal 2009.

Farkas has given readings throughout Canada, USA, Europe and Latin America. His poems have been translated into French, Spanish, Hungarian, Italian, Slovenian and Turkish.

CAROLYN MARIE SOUAID has been writing and publishing poetry for over twenty years. The author of six books and the winner of the David McKeen Award for her first collection, *Swimming into the Light*, she has also been shortlisted for the A.M. Klein Prize and the Pat Lowther Memorial Award.

Much of her work deals with the bridging of worlds; the difficulty, perhaps the impossibility of it, but the necessity of the struggle. She has toured her work across Canada and in France.

Since the 1990s, she has been a key figure on the Montreal literary scene, having co-produced two major local events, Poetry in Motion (the poetry-on-the-buses project) and Circus of Words/Cirque des mots, a multidisciplinary, multilingual cabaret focusing on the "theatre" of poetry. Souaid is a founding member and editor of *Poetry Quebec*, an online magazine dedicated to the English-language poets and poetry of Quebec.

ACKNOWLEDGEMENTS

We would like to acknowledge the many people who helped shape this DVD/book by bringing their own vision and expertise to the project. Not to mention long hours. Thanks to videographer and editor Martin Reisch (safe solvent), who brought the cemetery and black umbrellas to life; to soundscape artist Mark D. Goldman; to Jake Benjamin Shtern and Isabelle Rachel Shtern, the two children who were absolute pros in the studio. Still more thanks to J.P. Nault of DNA Productions, who turned the written text into the recorded word; and to our programmer and webmaster Elias Letelier, whose hard work on www.bloodisblood.com allows us to share in cyberspace a behind-the-scenes look at the four-year evolution of the project, making *Blood is Blood* a truly multi-media experience. Thanks to the Canada Council for the Arts for buying us time to develop the poem. Finally, a heartfelt appreciation to Karen Haughian, publisher of Signature Editions, who took a chance on this unusual book of poetry.